The Wonder Book of
COTTONTAILS
and Other Rabbits

By CYNTHIA ILIFF KOEHLER
and ALVIN KOEHLER

WONDER BOOKS · NEW YORK
A Division of GROSSET & DUNLAP, Inc.

First Library Edition Printed in 1974.

Library of Congress Catalog Card Number 73-16852
ISBN: 0-448-13190-0 (Library Edition)
1974 PRINTING

Every Mr. Cottontail has his favorite hideaway. It is easy to pass by without seeing him at all. But when he runs, you can see his funny little ball of cottontail bobbing up and down.

Mr. Cottontail has very big ears that he can turn around to catch the tiniest whisper of a sound. His large brown eyes can see in front or to the side or back, and even look up to the sky where his enemies, the hawks, may be.

A rabbit eats so fast that you can't see his teeth; but if you could see them, you would find that they are not just like yours. Mr. Cottontail has four very long teeth in front.

They are strong enough to chew dried corn and the bark of trees. What is even better for him, they keep growing in as he wears them away. He also has smaller teeth behind the big ones.

A rabbit never really walks, the way a cat or dog does. He hops or leaps, instead. His long back legs are like built-in springboards. He can take flying leaps of ten or fifteen feet.

When you see a rabbit run across a field, you may think he has no home at all. But every rabbit has a special area that he calls home. He knows every inch of it. First, he learns every place where he can hide — a hollow stump, a hole in the ground, a clump of bushes, or a pile of stones.

He knows where his favorite foods grow — the pink clover, the plantain with big leaves, and the trees with tender bark.

When he races off, he usually only runs to the end of his home ground, then he circles back again.

After the snows melt in March, the rabbits have gay parties. They run and jump in wild games of tag and leapfrog in the misty light of early morning. There are boxing matches and games of hide and seek. They forget the cold winter months and have all the fun they can before the busy days of summer.

On sunny spring days, every Mrs. Cottontail begins to look for the best place to make a nest for her babies. She wants a warm, dry place with a hideaway nearby. She digs a hole in the ground big enough to hold a family of four or five baby rabbits.

Then she gathers dry grass and soft leaves, and pats them in the hole. She pulls the softest fur from her neck and tummy to line the nest. This will make the softest, warmest kind of bed for her babies. She even makes a lid of dried grass to cover and hide the nest.

When a baby cottontail is born, he is very tiny and pink. He has no fur and his eyes and ears are tightly shut, so he isn't pretty at all. Mrs. Cottontail always stays nearby to feed and wash her little babies.

They grow so fast that in a week's time they are
beautiful tiny bunnies with brown fur and a dash of white
on each little brown head. Their ears grow and their brown
eyes open.

When baby cottontails are about two weeks old, they peek out of their nest at the big world around them. Soon, they crawl out to nibble clover and play. Mrs. Cottontail always watches them from her hideaway. She sniffs the air and listens for rabbit enemies. The babies learn to hide when she stomps her feet.

They begin to wash their faces, ears, and paws. They learn what plants make the best salads for growing rabbits.

The baby rabbits grow very fast during the summer months. By the time fall comes, all the rabbits are eating second helpings of food so they will be fat and have thick, warm fur for the cold days ahead.

Some animals crawl into holes and sleep through the winter — but not the rabbits. They take naps in their hideaways in the daytime, but when evening comes they go out to look for food. Their winter salads are bark and twigs, and seeds not covered by the snow.

Mountain Cottontail

Eastern Cottontail   Swamp Cottontail   Western Cottontail

The cottontail rabbits live in all parts of America — in deserts and swamps, in gardens and woods. The swamp rabbits can swim.

Don't try to catch wild rabbits for pets. They are happy only when they are free to run in gardens and fields.

English Lop Rabbit

Angora Rabbit   Black Dutch Rabbit   English Spot Rabbit

If you want a soft little rabbit for a pet, buy one of the
tame variety. There are some very pretty kinds, and they
make gentle pets. Find out just what sort of house and
food they need.

The famous Jack Rabbits with their great big ears and feet are not rabbits; they are cousins of the rabbits called hares. The Snowshoe Rabbits that have brown fur in summer and white fur in winter are also hares.